BEYOND THE BLUE

A Quest Into the Unknown!

Phillippa Leslie

UK Book Publishing.com

Cover artwork by Phillippa Leslie

Design, typesetting and publishing by UK Book Publishing

www.ukbookpublishing.com

ISBN: 978-1-916572-38-6

BEYOND THE BLUE

Books by the same author

Far From Plain Sailing
(An autobiography)

Jesus, Religion & Spirituality
(A Challenging Observation of Religions
and Beliefs Around the World)

Angelina the Clumsy Fairy
&
Animal Adventures
(A Collection of Nine Children's Short Stories)

The Open Road
(A Collection of Poems to Lighten the Soul
And Instil Hope and Courage)

FOREWORD

I have written this book to enlighten everyone (or those who are kind enough, and curious enough, to read it) to the possibility that there just might be something in it after all, and to be prepared!

I have attempted to cover only a very small portion of the astounding phenomena that has been found to exist, not only on our planet Earth, but in the vastness of the Universe, and in the depths of our oceans. We shall never know the extent of it, though continuous exploration of our incredible world carries on at a fast pace; even so, we shall *always* be left in wonder. Our universe is an enigma, no beginning and no end, infinite in all directions. The clue to the origins of everything can be found out there, and everything in nature has its own vibration. I wonder if we will be celebrated by future generations or perhaps be 'damned'!

Things we thought were impossible, and viewed with a highly sceptical approach, amounting to ridicule, are now becoming a reality. We are going to have to adjust to a different world and become more open-minded to the possibility that we may be facing unearthly encounters with beings of a far superior intelligence, that previously, with our closed minds, we never believed existed. It is time to question where we came from, why we are here, and where we are going!

Strangely, there has been an increase in UFO sightings before extreme weather disasters such as floods, hurricanes, tornados, drought, famine and plague. Could this be alien intervention, a warning perhaps that our planet will not be sustainable for much longer. It is definitely too late, however hard we try, to counteract the damage we have done to our beautiful world.

The megalithic structures, standing stones, stone circles, pyramids etc., could never have been built without help from another source, who had the knowledge and expertise that came from another dimension. Men have tried to replicate the building of such structures but have failed miserably. It cannot be done!

I am not the only Leslie in my very large family to be fascinated with extra-terrestrial phenomena and the unknown, and to be interested in the exploration of it. A rather distant relative, Desmond Leslie of Castle Leslie, Glaslough, Co. Monahan, in Ireland, worked with George

Adamski on the study of UFOs and the possibility of there being life on other planets, co-writing one of the first books on the subject, 'Flying Saucers Have Landed' in 1953. During his lifetime he served as a Spitfire pilot in the RAF during WWII, becoming one of the first pioneers of electronic music. He also wrote 'How Britain Won the Space Race' together with the late celebrated astronomer Patrick Moore.

George Adamski was a Polish/American author who became widely known for his interest, and apparent knowledge, of alien existence. He was the first, and most famous, of several UFO investigators who came to prominence during the 1950s. Patrick Moore was an English amateur astronomer who attained prominence in that field as a writer, radio commentator and television presenter.

CHAPTER 1

ALIENS ARE WE REALLY ALONE?

The answer to that is most emphatically 'NO'!

A few decades ago, belief in intelligent life beyond Earth was, more often than not, ridiculed. Today we have a very different story; it's more ridiculed *not* to believe it. Open your minds to the fantastical, the wondrous, the strange and beautiful, the frightening and ethereal phenomena that lures us, somewhat unwillingly, to confront the beckoning of alien hands.

Our understanding of the planets and Solar System grows, we are realizing that intelligent life must surely exist beyond our Earth. The beings who inhabit the skies will undoubtedly communicate in a different way to our many individual languages, and quite possibly through telepathy alone. In years to come we will have to adapt to a different existence (if we survive!) and quite possibly will begin to even look different, perhaps becoming some form of hybrid alien/human to adapt to a new environment. Our planet, as we very well know, is not going to be sustainable ad infinitum; we are going to have to change and possibly move from it altogether!

So far, we have been bamboozled into thinking aliens absolutely do not exist, and it all comes down to a 'weather balloon'! There has, in fact, been a very convincing 'cover-up' regarding possible sightings and UFO experiences. Not only the US military, but various military bodies in the UK, and countless everyday normal genuine people have been, not only quite terrified, but have recorded these events from as early as possibly 1946. It is on record that UFO's have been invading our airspace for thousands, possibly millions, of years without our knowledge, but nevertheless their presence has been felt more recently in various ways, and now we are having to accept that they are here. For all we know they may have been among us for some time, and I *do* mean among us! If we are honest, and face the possibility head on, we would definitely come to the conclusion that the probability of our being entirely alone in the universe is not logical. There must surely be numerous other planets to stimulate our future curiosity and to expand our knowledge through exploration. Jesus said "My father's house has many rooms"! We are purposefully closing our minds to the rather frightening possibility that other beings exist and are superior in intellect to us. ***Do we really know what we think we know?***

For example, we as humans live by a code of ethics whereby to cross over into experimenting with cross genetics, involving the fusing of animals and humans to produce a hybrid entity, is to us totally abhorrent. However, how do we know that it has not been done elsewhere, and that these mutations inhabit perhaps another planet? Man is naturally curious, and I find it quite hard to believe that curiosity has not inevitably out manoeuvred ethics, and that unbeknown to us experiments such as this are currently being carried out. We, in actual fact, are already experimenting with cross genetics, with dogs in particular, producing miniature hybrids for sale as a 'designer' breed. Scientists in China have produced a 'pig-monkey' as part of research into the growth of human organs for plantation in animals. Could the creatures of our nightmares actually exist? It would seem quite likely.

In ancient cave paintings and rock and stone carvings, which have been discovered through exploration by scientists and archaeologists etc., the gods and figures depicted therein appear to be totally 'alien' to us, but how do we know that at one time, tens of thousands of years' ago, they did not exist? They appear to be 'monsters' of rather frightening and bizarre appearance, but they could very well have actually existed, and in many regions around the globe these 'gods' are very much part of peoples' everyday lives, their effigies being revered and prayed to on a regular basis.

We are familiar with television personalities such as the late Patrick Moore and now Brian Cox (professor of particle physics in the School of Physics & Astronomy at Manchester University) studying the stars, the galaxies and planets, and the recent discovery of 'black holes', 'worm holes', and 'portals'. Exploration of these intangible and ethereal phenomena in the future will bring us closer to understanding where we have come from and where we are going. We are seeking all the time the meaning of life; *is* there life out there on another planet? Our brave astronauts fly in rockets to the moon, risking their lives to find the answers. They too have looked out of the windows of their capsule to witness strange lights shooting past them, and to have seen possible outcrops of buildings on the dark side of the moon. Are these sightings possibly alien military bases, and actually inhabited? Further exploration will undoubtedly tell us in the years to come.

Humans have long dreamed of going into space, and now the wealthiest and most famous can buy the chance to make this a reality. This new space craze began in 2013 when Richard Branson, the CEO of spaceflight company Virgin Galactic, announced he was selling seats for sub-orbital flight that would take guests 50 miles into Earth's atmosphere to the edge of space, all in the span of a few minutes. Many celebrities have purchased tickets to fly on an upcoming space flight. Perhaps this will become the next exciting adventure on the 'bucket list' of the super-rich, possibly becoming common place excursions for all of us in the future!

Past US presidents have acknowledged the fact that alien craft and their crew, although perhaps being an entity or species to appease and befriend, are also definitely a force to fear. Their obvious superior intelligence is beyond our understanding. These past Presidents and countless others have acknowledged that they *do* exist! Presidents Eisenhower, Truman, Nixon, Carter, Reagan, Kennedy and Obama, not only witnessed UFO phenomena, but *all* acknowledged that there is 'something' inhabiting our skies that we do not understand, and undoubtedly should be wary of, and have attempted to gain more explicit knowledge of the unidentified craft and their crew invading our airspace.

The aliens have come to be known as 'the Greys'. They are not little green men, but the shape of their very thin bodies, large heads and extra-large almond shaped eyes we are reasonably familiar with, their bodies being grey, not green. Most attempts to uncover information have been thwarted, and those intent on enquiring having been fobbed off with irrational and rather ridiculous explanations, all so-called 'sightings' and other phenomena being highly classified and strictly off limits.

Bodies of these Greys have nevertheless been extricated from several UFOs that have crashed, and are stored at the US Military Base of Area 51 along with the remains of the vehicles they came in. This base is approximately 83 miles north/north west of Las Vegas in the Nevada desert in California, and heavily guarded.

The UFOs that have been witnessed to date are of various shapes and sizes, the obvious ones being saucer shaped, but others have been seen to be diamond shaped, oblong, triangular with flashing coloured lights, and other sightings merely single lights or clusters of coloured lights moving at speed, that literally dance through the sky. They have been reported hovering over Military bases, maybe to glean information, and sometimes to shut them down completely! In 1952 a cluster of UFOs flew over the White House in Washington DC, being witnessed by literally hundreds of people.

The US and British Military, particularly pilots, have definitely encountered UFOs, having been seriously unnerved when an unidentified flying craft has completely de-activated the controls, leaving the 'plane in a 'gliding' state. As soon as the craft flew off, the controls appeared to re-activate. Pilots have also chased and been chased by these flying craft, and been hopelessly outrun, the immense speed of the craft having been totally beyond their ability to follow, and far advanced of anything we might possess to counter an attack. When pilots have attempted to attack, what they believe to be alien enemy aircraft, ammunition has literally 'bounced' off and made no impact at all. *Friend or Foe? We do not know!*

US and UK Military pilots claim that Aliens are sabotaging British and US nuclear missiles. Former US airman Capt. Robert Salas previously reported that "The US Air Force is lying about the national security implications of unidentified aerial objects at nuclear bases and we can prove it". He said that he witnessed such an event first-hand on March 16th 1967, at Malmstrom Air Force Base in Montana which housed Minuteman nuclear missiles. Capt.

Salas continued: "I was on duty when an object came over and hovered directly over the site. The missiles shut down – 10 Minuteman missiles! And the same thing happened at another site a week later. There's a strong interest in our missiles by these objects, wherever they come from. I personally think they're not from planet Earth". As well as the control panel being rendered completely inoperative, the missiles were then activated to within the point of launch, but were then miraculously shut down at the last minute, and the UFOs disappeared. This brings us to the obvious conclusion that alien forces are completely capable of disabling any nuclear armaments we possess, meaning that *our planet is undoubtedly at their mercy, and our future lies in their hands.*

Others claim to have seen similar activity in the UK. Col. Charles Halt said he saw a UFO at the former Military Base RAF Bentwaters, near Ipswich, 30 years' ago, during which time he saw beams of light fired into the base, then heard on the military radio that aliens had landed inside the nuclear storage area.

He said: "I believe that the security services of both the United States and the United Kingdom have attempted, both then and now, to subvert the significance of what occurred at RAF Bentwaters by the use of well-practised methods of disinformation". The site was then the base of the US 81st Tactical Fighter Wing.

Capt. Bruce Fenstermacher, a former US Air Force officer, also claims he saw a cigar-shaped UFO hovering above a nuclear base in Wyoming in 1976.

These are bona fide military personnel, and their credibility is beyond doubt, likewise the credibility of the aforesaid US Presidents.

What is unfolding before us is so bizarre and fantastical that it would appear to echo scenes from a Sci-Fi movie. However, it *is* happening. It is not just daunting but wholly unnerving to have to come to terms with the knowledge that, far from not being alone, an alien species exists that is far superior in intellect than we as humans profess to be. We are now being given a warning that not only are we destroying our environment but are inventing ourselves out of the equation! Artificial intelligence is undoubtedly rushing to the fore, and human interaction becoming less and less required. *What then? Where do we go? Who are we?* People of considerable intellect and impeccable character, such as astrophysicists, archaeologists, scientists, university professors, military personnel, pilots, governmental bodies, police forces, American presidents, and people going about their normal everyday lives, are reporting sightings of UFOs, lights in the sky and terrifying abductions, affording actual contact with the Greys. So far abductions have seemed to consist of experiments being performed on humans, and in some cases tiny implants under the surface of the skin have been detected after the event, containing some sort of code. It seems they have a specific agenda, that being to carry out various experiments (for what reason we do not yet know) and to analyse the general fundamental qualities of character, and physical construction, pertaining to the human race. These experiments do not apply to just humans but also to animals. Cattle and sheep have been found mutilated, having had parts of their bodies removed with what appears to be surgical precision, as though with some kind of laser.

History, in various forms, has documented unusual and extraordinary sightings of lights and craft in the skies that local people, in numerous regions of the world, have experienced. We, being secure in the knowledge of our superiority and uniqueness, and with a considerable degree of arrogance, have not only been reluctant to acknowledge interference from anything extra-terrestrial, but have flatly refused to believe it to be possible, and the fact that we are actually living on a 'planet' has never really sunk in, or been of much importance; the fact that we are all part of the universe. Our bodies contain the knowledge of the universe, and the particles making us up have been around since the beginning of time. We don't question why we look the way we do, what we are actually made of, and of course what we are doing here in the first place. We just 'are'! This planet is not ours, we are merely caretakers, and therefore have a grave responsibility to not only care for it, but to enrich it for future generations to enjoy. Suddenly we are having to wake up to the enormity of the possibility that, if we are not immediately mindful of our fate, *we are in danger of literally being wiped out.*

Floods, hurricanes, tornadoes, famine, earthquakes and drought are now part of our daily existence, becoming extreme in intensity, and we are now having to admit that our planet is definitely becoming warmer with a more Mediterranean feel. Pollution is rife and unstoppable; we are running out of space, and the means with which to solve this ever-growing problem. How can we possibly cleanse our seas of the plastic endangering the vulnerable species of life within it, or eradicate the foul stench of so-called 'progress' in the mounds of imperishable rubbish blotting the landscape? The populace at large are now faced with the virtually impossible task of trying to solve this appalling state of our once naturally beautiful world. Scientists in the past invented our way of life to the point of our being totally reliant on man-made and durable materials; so durable in fact that we now have this horrendous and deadly problem of being unable to rectify it.

CHAPTER 2

THE PRESIDENTS

President Dwight D Eisenhower (Ike)

In 1953 President Harry Truman relinquished his position in the oval office and handed the reins of power to his successor, President Dwight D. Eisenhower. Along with the transition came an extensive file concerning a top secret project called Majestic 12 that President Truman had established. Majestic 12 consisted of a group of scientists, governmental professionals and military personnel who worked together to understand and communicate with UFOs and extra-terrestrial beings.

The MJ-12 saga begins with the alleged crash and recovery of an alien spacecraft near Roswell, New Mexico. President Truman instructed the Secretary of Defence James Forrestal to set up Operation Majestic Twelve, a Top Secret panel headed by Vannever Bush. Researchers contend that the MJ-12 brokered a meeting between extra-terrestrials and President Eisenhower, during which an agreement was reached to allow alien studies of human biology through abductions and animal mutilations in exchange for the use of extra-terrestrial 'black technology' that would lead to developments such as the B-2 'Stealth Bomber'.

President Eisenhower was fascinated and extremely interested in UFOs and extra-terrestrials and it is documented that he met with these beings secretly, several times. Once at Edwards Air Force Base in California and twice at Holloman Air Force Base in New Mexico. Several other instances of UFOs landing at or near Holloman have been reported since the Eisenhower meetings.

Eisenhower had been a five-star Army general, therefore not a figure to be questioned on his integrity. In February 1954 he spent several days in Palm Springs on holiday, and disappearing for several hours one Saturday afternoon, missed a scheduled public dinner. He was not seen again until late the following morning. His whereabouts were questioned by the Press and they were told that he had an emergency appointment with a dentist for a chipped tooth. The story was later dismissed as being a cover-up, and it was rumoured that he had been visiting ETs at nearby Edwards Air Force Base.

There were records of people who met the aeroplane, people who sent flowers, the minister who gave the sermon at the Sunday service he attended, and anyone else who had played any kind of role in his entourage, but there was absolutely no record of any 'dentist appointment', and years later the dentist's widow revealed that her husband had never mentioned that he had ever done dental work on the President.

William Cooper, who was on the Naval Intelligence briefing team and had access to classified documents, revealed that ETs had had contact with Earth. They had warned that the Earth was 'on a path of self-destruction' and they wanted to meet to help in establishing a long-lasting peace.

President Eisenhower's first meeting with the aliens occurred at Edwards Air Force Base in February 1954. A Naval Commander, Charles Suggs reported that his father had attended the meeting between Ike and the ETs who appeared to be blue-eyed. The discussions were polite and 'peaceful', and Eisenhower, although wanting to effect a treaty with the aliens, was not willing to agree to their demand that we cease testing nuclear weapons. The aliens left without an agreement regarding a treaty, but returned the following year to the Holloman base in New Mexico for a subsequent meeting with Eisenhower.

In February 1955 approximately 300 people saw Air Force One land at Holloman Air Force Base and taxi back out to the end of the runway. Shortly after the plane landed, the pilot instructed the tower to turn off all radar while the President's plane was on the tarmac. Shortly after Air Force One landed, and the radar was turned off, three round objects were seen in the sky. One landed about 200 feet in front of Air Force One, another hovered over the area as though keeping watch, and a third one disappeared from visibility. A man, presumed to be Eisenhower, descended the steps of Air Force One. He was then seen shaking hands with a being at the door of the UFO subsequently entering the space craft. He was in the space craft for about 45 minutes. As he was not wearing his hat on leaving, everyone identified him as being President Eisenhower.

The upshot is that these particular extra-terrestrials apparently wanted peace and were trying to negotiate some sort of positive outcome for Earth's many problems, wanting the public to be told the truth about their existence, though seemed to change their minds later.

Ultimately, Eisenhower 'signed a Treaty' with an alien race called Alien Greys, the terms of the Treaty being:

- *We would not be involved in their affairs and they would not become involved in ours*
- *They would help us with developing our technology*
- *They would not make a treaty with any other nation on Earth*
- *They could abduct humans for various experiments, but had to provide names of all those they abducted to Earth's Majestic 12 committee*
- *The public would not be informed about the existence of ETs*

President Richard Nixon

Almost half a century ago Nixon supposedly had earth shattering evidence that the US government possessed advanced scientific knowledge gleaned from aliens, and what he chose to do with it was hide it in a time capsule. Nixon allegedly shared this revelation with only two people, Robert Merritt, a sometime police informant and covert domestic intelligence operative for the Nixon administration (he said he was shown proof of extra-terrestrial life during a meeting with the President), and the other person privy to this information was his National Security Adviser Henry Kissinger, who has never spoken of the matter. Nixon said that whatever nation possessed this advanced knowledge could 'rule the world'.

President James Earl Carter, Jnr

Future President Jimmy Carter filed a report with the National Investigations Committee on Aerial Phenomena on September 18th 1973, claiming he had seen an Unidentified Flying Object in October 1969.

During the presidential campaign of 1975, Carter was forthcoming about his belief that he had seen a UFO. He described waiting outside the venue for a Lion's Club meeting to begin in Leary, Georgia, at around 7.30 p.m. when he spotted what he called "the darndest thing I've ever seen" in the sky. Carter, as well as 10 to 12 other people also witnessed the same event. They described the object as "very bright with changing colours and about the size of the moon". Carter reported that "the object hovered about 30 degrees above the horizon and moved in towards the earth then away before disappearing into the distance".

He promised that, if elected president, he would encourage the government to release every piece of information pertaining to UFO's, therefore making it available to both the public and scientists. However, after winning the presidency, he backed away from this pledge, saying that the release of this information might possibly have defence implications and pose a threat to national security.

President Ronald Reagan

In 1974 the Governor of California, Ronald Reagan, was a passenger in a Cessna Citation aircraft approaching Bakersfield, California. On board were the pilot Bill Paynter and two security guards. On approaching Bakersfield the passengers called Paynter's attention to a strange object flying to their rear. "It appeared to be several hundred yards away" Paynter recalled. "It was a fairly steady light until it began to accelerate. Then it appeared to elongate. Then the light took off. It went up at a 45-degree angle, at a high rate of speed. Everyone on the plane was surprised. The

UFO went from a normal cruise speed to a fantastic speed instantly. If you give an airplane power, it will accelerate, but not like a hot rod, and that's what this was like".

President Reagan had a fascination with Science Fiction and consequently UFOs; anything relating to extra-terrestrial contact being of great interest to him. At the 1985 Geneva Summit, President Reagan and Soviet Premier Mikhail Gorbachev took a break from negotiations and went for a walk. Only their private interpreters were present, and for years the details of what they discussed were kept secret from both the Russian and American public. But apparently, during an interview in 2009 Gorbachev revealed that Reagan asked him point-blank if they could set aside their differences in case the world was invaded by aliens.

President John Fitzgerald Kennedy

Ten days before Kennedy's assassination, secret documents had been uncovered revealing that he had written to the head of the CIA demanding to be shown highly confidential documents with regard to UFOs. A possible theory with regard to his assassination is that his interest was not welcome, which may have prompted his 'removal'. Alien researchers say that the latest documents, released by the CIA, add weight to the suggestion that the president could have been shot to stop him discovering the truth about UFOs.

Conspiracy theorists add interest to a disputed file nicknamed the 'burned memo', which a UFO investigator claims he received in the 1990's. The document, which has scorch marks, is claimed to have been mailed to UFO hunter Timothy Cooper in 1999 by an unknown CIA leak, but has never been verified. In a note sent with the document, the person who revealed it said he worked for the CIA between 1960 and 1974, and pulled the memo from a fire when the agency was burning some of its most sensitive files. The undated memo contained a reference to 'Lancer', which was JFK's Secret Service code name.

On the first page, the director of Central Intelligence wrote: 'As you must know, Lancer has made some inquiries regarding our activities, which we cannot allow. Please submit your views no later than October. Your action to this matter is critical to the continuance of the group'.

UFO investigator Robert Wood said that he had engaged a forensics company to check the age of the paper, the ink, watermarks, font types and other markings, using the same techniques normally used in a court of law. The conclusion being that the memo was authentic.

It is thought that Marilyn Monroe gained information regarding UFOs from her close association with JFK. There has been suspicion surrounding her death ever since, as to whether it was, in fact, an act to silence her.

Barak Obama

Former President Barak Obama has commented on videos of unidentified aerial phenomena which have continued to gain attention, not only in the United States but all over the western world.

"What is true, and I'm actually being serious here, is that there is footage and records of objects in the skies, and we don't know what exactly they are" he said. "They did not have an easily explainable pattern, and so I think that people still take it seriously, trying to investigate and figure out what they are!

Prince Philip

The late Prince Philip, Duke of Edinburgh, was fascinated with UFOs and close encounters. He was a regular subscriber of 'Flying Saucer Review' a quarterly magazine established in 1955.

He first developed an interest in UFOs from his uncle Lord Mountbatten, who wrote an official report about a space craft that reportedly landed on his estate in Romsey, Hampshire, in 1955.

Philip had given his former assistant Sir Peter Horsley 'carte blanche' to collect stories of UFOs from the RAF. Horsley wrote about a close encounter with an 'alien' in London in 1954, and said he was asked to bring witnesses to

Buckingham Palace for private discussions with the Duke.

In 2019 Philip read 'The Halt Perspective', written by retired US Air Force Col. Charles Halt, a former deputy Commander of RAF Bentwaters, who described how he had led a patrol to investigate an alleged UFO landing in the Rendlesham Forest in 1980. The incident was dubbed 'Britain's Roswell' after the famous crash of a US Army Air Force balloon in New Mexico in 1947.

CHAPTER 3

INCREDIBLE BRAINS OF THE PAST

Leonardo da Vinci

Leonardo di ser Piero da Vinci was born near Florence in 1452. His parents were unmarried, and although he possessed this amazing mind he actually never went to school. He was left-handed and often wrote from right to left in a 'mirror' style, where the reader would have to read what he had written with the use of a mirror. In actual fact, he was the only one who could correctly decipher it. He was a huge lover of animals as can be seen from the many remarkable and beautiful drawings we can now appreciate.

He was able to see the future to the point of prophecy, foreseeing and inventing many complex physical artefacts that we now take completely for granted. We call him 'a genius' today, but where did this incredible knowledge come from? Did he receive information from another source? Did he visit the future through 'time travel'? His gift to mankind is truly a gift to the world. Apparently, he disappeared for two years – where did he go? Sigmund Freud wrote: "He was like a man who awoke too early in the darkness while the others were all still asleep". Is it possible that he may have used this technique to hide messages within the painting of the Mona Lisa? She is said to have been a portrait of the wife of a Florentine official.

Da Vinci's numerous fantastic inventions and predictions of their future deployment were numerous:

THE TANK

His first was a War Tank, but ironically he designed them to go backwards instead of forwards, perhaps in the hope that they would not actually be used in an act of war, being a pacifist himself. He took his inspiration from a turtle shell! It was designed to move in any direction and came equipped with a number of light cannons. Like many of his inventions the idea was simply fantastical, as it couldn't possibly have been realized at the time he thought it up, the materials not having been invented. This was not the only military equipment.

THE MACHINE GUN

He also created a 'machine gun' which was the inventor's solution to the problem of gun cannons taking too long to load. In theory one row would fire as another would cool and a third would load, so that soldiers could fire on their enemies without interruption.

THE SUBMARINE

Da Vinci had the idea that ships could possibly travel underwater, and even sketched designs for this type of vessel. On realizing how dangerous this could be in the wrong hands, da Vinci kept this design secret "because of the evil nature of men who practice assassination at the bottom of the sea".

THE HELICOPTER

The 'aerial screw', essentially a man-powered helicopter, was another of da Vinci's fantastical inventions dreamt up, but again impossible to bring into reality requiring materials and technology that had not yet been discovered.

THE REFRIGERATOR

Da Vinci not only thought about human flight and warfare. He also predicted a number of practical appliances for the home i.e. a 'cooling machine', now of course known as the refrigerator. He predicted this incredible, and extremely useful, technology long before anyone even began considering the need for it.

THE PARACHUTE

Da Vinci also thought up an early version of the parachute. His vision was made of sealed linen cloth and was held up by wooden poles. Although this idea was very primitive and would definitely have been far too heavy to fly, it was however the first attempt at man's desire to take to the skies unaided except by wind and a piece of cloth.

EVOLUTION

Long before Charles Darwin caused a major uproar with his theory of evolution, da Vinci had much the same idea. In fact, he apparently took the idea that humans had evolved from apes as a foregone conclusion, and didn't really try to argue it. He was fascinated with the human body and its parts, and every conceivable bone, artery, muscle and vein would be meticulously recorded and drawn time and time again to achieve perfection.

SOLAR POWER

Harnessing the power of the sun da Vinci designed his own solar power system to heat water for Florence. While he was working at the Vatican da Vinci experimented with 'burning mirrors' and predicted that these concave deflective devices could be used to focus sunlight and harness it. These mirrors were used to heat water.

CALCULATOR

Many credit da Vinci with the invention of the calculator. A hundred years before German Wilhelm Schikard built his 'calculating clock' da Vinci sketched out plans for a calculating apparatus of his own.

TELESCOPE

When people automatically think of Galileo as having invented the telescope before da Vinci, the latter may actually have predicted the eventual creation of the telescope a century earlier. He reportedly wrote "Make eyeglasses to see the moon larger".

ROBOTS

Da Vinci also designed what might have been the very first humanoid robot. His 'armoured knight' was capable of sitting up, waving its arms, moving its head and opening and closing its jaw. This robotic knight was made up of a suit that was filled with various gears and wheels connected to a pulley and cable system, which enabled the 'robot' to move on its own.

Nostradamus

Michel de Nostradame was born in Saint-Remy-de-Provence, France in 1503. He was one of 9 children born to Reyniere de St. Remey and Jaume de Nostradame, a well-to-do grain dealer of part Jewish descent.

He was exceptionally intelligent from a very early age, quickly advancing through school. He was taught Latin, Greek, Hebrew and Mathematics. His grandfather, Jean de St. Remy, also taught him the rudiments of astrology, giving Nostradamus his first exposure to the idea of the heavens and how they might influence human destiny. He received licence to practice medicine in 1952, and at this time he latinized his name from Nostradame to Nostradamus.

Nostradamus developed some very progressive methods for dealing with bubonic plague, which had previously brought death and misery to his country.

An off-handed remark regarding a religious statue resulted in charges of heresy again Nostradamus. When ordered to appear before the inquisition, he wisely chose to leave Provence to travel for several years through Italy, Greece and Turkey. He eventually returned to Provence to resume his practice of treating plague victims. He married Anne Ponsarde and together they had six children.

Where did his incredible supernatural gift come from; did he have instruction and visual affirmation of things to come from a higher source? Was he in contact with other beings of superior knowledge, who had the ability to see beyond our human capacity, and to instruct and guide these gifted people into helping mankind to evolve at a faster pace than their otherwise lower form of intelligence would allow.

Nostradamus began publishing cryptic quatrains in 1555, but these were in the form of predictions and not ordinary poetry.

PREDICTIONS

He predicted the death of King Henry II:

> *The young lion will overcome the older one*
> *On the field of combat in a single battle*
> *He will pierce his eyes through a golden cage*
> *Two wounds made one, then he dies a cruel death*

In the summer of 1559 King Henry II (older one) lined up to joust Gabriel, Comte de Montgomery (young lion) six years his junior. In the final pass Montgomery's lance burst through the king's visor (he will pierce his eyes through a golden cage) and splintered. The profusely bleeding king remained conscious and was able to walk. However, splinters from the lance had entered the king's eye, throat, and temple (two wounds made one). Henry experienced agonizing pain, seizures, and partial paralysis (*he dies a cruel death*) before finally dying in his bed eleven days later.

NAPOLEON

> *Pau, Nay, Loron will be more of fire than of blood*
> *To swim in praise, the great one to flee to the confluence*
> *He will refuse entry to the Piuse*
> *The depraved ones and the Durance*
> *will keep them imprisoned*

Pau, Nay, Loron are three towns in southern France; Pau, Nay and Oloron.

The fascinating re-arrangement of these letters spells out NAPAULON ROY or Napoleon the King in French.

(More of the fire than of the blood) refers to Napoleon's humble lineage, and the *(refuse entry to the Piuses)* relates to Popes Pius VI and VII, both imprisoned by Napoleon.

THE REIGN OF KING PHILIP OF SPAIN

For seven years Philip's fortune will prosper
He will reduce the Arab army
Then halfway through, things will
perplexedly turn against him
A young onion will destroy his fortune

King Philip of Spain commenced ruling the country in 1556 and Spain became exceptionally wealthy for the first years of his reign. "Seven" could possibly mean the biblical translation of a "long time". However, in 1587, with the execution of Mary Queen of Scots, who was also Catholic, his success came to an abrupt halt. Her death effectively ended his alliance with England. A year later he attempted to invade England with his Spanish Armada fleet of ships, but was thwarted in this undertaking.

The "young onion" refers to the 36-year-old Henry IV of France, a Huguenot, and thus a Protestant. He and Philip disagreed on religion and battled until Henry's death.

LOUIS PASTEUR

The lost thing is discovered, hidden for many centuries
Pasteur will be celebrated almost as a God-like figure
This is when the moon completes her great cycle
But by other rumours he shall be dishonoured

Born in 1822, Louis Pasteur was a French chemist and microbiologist who discovered that the growth of micro-organisms causes fermentation. That discovery also proved that bacteria does not simply appear spontaneously as previously thought. Instead, it grows from already living organisms in a process called biogenesis.

While Pasteur did not first propose 'germ theory', he convinced much of Europe of its validity. He invented a process for removing bacteria, 'pasteurization', which is named after him. His early work also led to the invention of vaccines for rabies and anthrax.

However, in 1995, Gerald Geison, a science historian, published a book revealing that Pasteur incorporated a rival's findings to make his anthrax vaccine functional. That finding partly 'dishonoured' the great scientist, as Nostradamus predicted.

ADOLF HITLER

From the depths of the West of Europe
A child will be born of poor people
He who by his tongue will seduce a great troop
His fame will increase towards the realm of the East

Also:

Beasts ferocious with hunger will cross the rivers
The greater part of the battlefield will be against Hister

Into a cage of iron will the great one be drawn
When the child of Germany observes nothing

On April 20th 1889 Adolf Hitler was born in Austria, Western Europe. Although his family were middle class they were not impoverished.

Hitler rose to power partly due to his oratory skills *(by his tongue will seduce)* rallying an army who showed powerful allegiance to 'der fuhrer', initiating WWII *(a great troop)* by invading Poland.

Although some Nastradamus supporters believe that Hister is a miss-spelling of Hitler, it is also the Latin word for the river Danube.

CHARLES DE GAULLE

Hercules King of Rome and of Annemark
With the surname of the chief of triple Gaul
Italy and the one of St. Mark to tremble
First monarch, renowned above all

Charles de Gaulle was three times leader of France *(chief of triple Gaul)*. Initially, de Gaulle led the Free French Forces during WWII. He then became prime minister of the provisional post WWII government. Lastly, de Gaulle was the first president of the French Fifth Republic.

HIROSHIMA & NAGASAKI

Near the gates and within two cities
There will be scourges the like of which was never seen
Famine within plague, people put out by steel
Crying to the great immortal God for relief

In early August 1945 the United States of America dropped two atomic bombs on the island of Japan; on Hiroshima and Nagasaki *(within two cities)*. The cities were annihilated and many survivors of the blast suffered horrifying radiation poisoning *(crying to the great immortal God for relief)*.

In the aftermath of the war, Japan experienced a food shortage crisis *(famine within plague)*.

THE ASSASSINATION OF PRESIDENT JOHN F. KENNEDY AND BOBBY KENNEDY

The great man will be struck down by a thunderbolt
An evil deed foretold by the bearer of a petition
According to the prediction another falls at night time
Conflict at Reims, London and pestilence in Tuscany

President John Kennedy *(great man)* received numerous death threats *(petition)* over the course of his presidency. When visiting Dallas on November 22 1963, the president was gunned down whilst being driven in an open car with his wife beside him *(thunderbolt)*. The shock devastated the nation and the whole western world.

His brother Bobby Kennedy was later also assassinated just after midnight on June 5 1968 (another falls at night time).

The conflict in Reims and London and sickness in Tuscany does not seem to bear much resemblance to any events that have been recognized.

TWIN TOWERS NEW YORK CITY

Earth shaking fire from the centre of the Earth
Will cause tremors around New City
Two great rocks war for a long time
Then Arethusa will redden a new river

On the morning of September 11 2001, the twin towers *(two great rocks)* of the World Trade Centre in New York City *(New City)* collapsed after al-Qaeda terrorists crashed hijacked passenger 'planes into the two buildings. Nostradamus' prediction with regard to 'Arethusa will redden a new river' does not seem to connect with the above.

Albert Einstein

Albert Einstein is the most influential physicist of the 20th century, and quite possibly the most famous scientist who ever lived. In 1905, at the age of only 26, he published four papers electrifying the field of physics and propelling him to global recognition and renown. He is also remembered for his quick wit and incredible insights into humanity, knowledge and imagination, immortalized in his endless inspiring quotes.

His ground breaking special theory of relativity represented by mc 2, which could be turned into energy, was among his famous works. Not since mathematician Isaac Newton had one man altered our understanding of the Universe and how it works.

His schooling was in Munich, Germany, where he felt alienated and held back by the school's stunted approach to teaching. He was an average pupil though experienced speech difficulties which in the future influenced his view of education and human potential. Einstein was awarded the Nobel Prize for Physics in 1921, but history intervened. The Nazis were on the rise in his native Germany, and the Jewish Einstein became a target for assassination. He moved to the United States where he worked at Princeton University for the rest of his days. There, he became a central figure in the ensuing fight to curtail the use of the atom bomb and a strong voice against nationalism and racism. Einstein has become synonymous with genius and creativity. He was named a Person of the Century in 1999.

Again, who might have influenced this incredible brain, where insights into yet unknown theories became known to the world? He did not adhere to our conventional ideas of a 'tidy' appearance, but discarded ties and socks for old sweaters, crumpled trousers, and rather well-worn shoes!

He extended beyond science to reveal almost a childlike sense of wonder and a profound love of humanity. His quotes are famous and give us inspiration and affirmation in our lives.

EINSTEIN QUOTES:

The following are just a few of the many inspirational and life-enhancing quotes written by Einstein during his lifetime:

Imagination is more important than knowledge.
Knowledge is limited, imagination encircles the world.

A man should look for what is, and not
for what he thinks should be.

I believe in intuitions and inspirations. I sometimes
feel that I am right. I do not know that I am.

I have no special talent; I am only passionately curious.

Imagination is everything. It is the preview
of life's coming attractions.

He who can no longer pause to wonder and stand rapt
in awe, is as good as dead; his eyes are closed.

Great spirits have always encountered violent opposition from mediocre minds.

If you want your children to be intelligent, read them fairy tales. If you want them to be more intelligent, read them more fairy tales.

Let us not forget that human knowledge and skills alone cannot lead humanity to a happy and dignified life.

Unthinking respect for authority is the greatest enemy of truth.

Try not to become a man of success, but rather try to become a man of value.

Two things are 'infinite'; the universe and human stupidity; and I'm not sure about the universe.

All religious, arts and sciences are branches of the same tree.

A clever person solves a problem. A wise person avoids lit.

Only a life lived for others is worthwhile.

The great moral teachers of humanity were, in a way, artistic geniuses in the art of living.

Reality is merely an illusion, albeit a very persistent one.

*Life is like riding a bicycle. To keep your
balance you must keep moving.*

I love to travel, but I hate to arrive.

*I speak to everyone in the same way, whether he is
the garbage man or the president of the university.*

**There are many more, but I think perhaps one might get a little
tired by the end!**

CHAPTER 4

ANCIENT ALIEN MEGALITHIC STRUCTURES

Planet Earth is home to some spectacular relics from bygone eras; constructions that seem to totally defy technological capabilities of their time, either because they are too big, too heavy or too complex. As such, it is suggested that the ancient buildings of the pyramids were built by those adhering to some extra- terrestrial intervention. Perhaps the hands that crafted these sites were not really of this world. The construction of all these amazing sites could not have been brought about by any form of man-made tool, as their positioning is breathtakingly accurate, and could only today be formed by laser precision, which was totally unheard of at that time. The evidence of extra-terrestrial existence is actually all around us, in the depiction of ancient alien beings carved into megalithic structures and free-standing huge stones. These extraordinary and bizarre figures may well once have lived and walked our earth. Some of these carvings have been found depicting figures resembling 'astronauts' with helmets and space suits!

SACSAYHUAMAN

Outside the old Inca capital of Cusco, a fortress called Sacsayhuaman rests in the Peruvian Andes, built from colossal stones that have been chiselled and stacked together like a giant jigsaw puzzle. These 1,000-year-old interlocking fortress walls are constructed of rocks that weigh as much as 360 tons each, and which were carried more than 20 miles before being lifted into incredibly accurate adjoining blocks with again, laser-like precision.

PUMA PUNKU

Puma Punku, which literally translated means 'Gate of the Puma', is a 6th century T-shaped man-made terraced platform mound with a sunken court, found at the Tiwanaku site near Tiwanaku in Western Bolivia.

Today, the Puma Punku complex is an alignment of ramps on a platform mound; it now lies in ruins. It is believed to date back to AD 536. At the site several miniature gates were found, being perfect replicas of the once standing full size gateways. In its original magnificence, it is thought to have been 'unimaginably wondrous' possibly adorned with polished metal plaques, brightly coloured ceramic and draped with coloured fabrics.

Tiwanaku is significant in Inca tradition because it is believed by them to be the site where the world was created.

There again, no-one can solve the amazing accuracy of the construction, begging the question of possible other worldly assistance and a superior knowledge of technique. The Inca people believe another highly intelligent civilisation preceded them and built their megalithic structures.

ABU SIMBEL EGYPT

Abu Simbel is a historic site comprising two massive rock cut temples in the village of Abu Simbel in Upper Egypt near the border of Sudan.

Deep within the interior of the Great Temple at Abu Simbel, and carved into a mountainside is southern Egypt's ancient Nubian Valley, a vast wondrous world. Intricate military artworks adorn pillars which support a ceiling painted with winged vultures. There are floor to ceiling hieroglyphics depicting victorious battles of Pharoah Ramses II, the man responsible for this enormous temple. Four colossal statues of the pharaoh face east towards the rising sun, overlooking a crystal-clear lake.

It is an incredible site of impeccable craftsmanship, and one can only wonder and view with awe at how they were able to achieve such an immense work of magnificence with again no modern tools, which inevitably makes one think that they surely must have had superior knowledge and instruction from a higher intelligence.

CHICHEN ITZA

Chichen Itza is a ruined ancient Mayan city covering an area of foursquare miles in the south-central Yucatan state in Mexico. It possibly would have been a religious, political or military centre and would have been home to 35,000 people. Settlers arrived in 550 AD, probably drawn there because of the easy access to water in the region via caves, sinkholes and limestone formations known as cenotes. The only source of water in the arid region around the site was from cenotes. Two big cenotes on the site made it a suitable place to build a city, and gave it its name *chi* meaning 'mouths', *chen* meaning 'wells' and Itza being the name of the tribe that settled there. The Maya are the most ancient civilisation on this planet.

STONEHENGE, SALISBURY, ENGLAND

Stonehenge is perhaps the world's most famous prehistoric monument. The first monument was an early henge monument, built some 5,000 years' ago, and the unique stone circle was created in the late Neolithic period at about 2,500BC. Many burial mounds were built nearby in the early Bronze age. Two types of stone are used at Stonehenge – the larger sarsens and the smaller bluestones. In about 2,500 BC the stones were set up in the centre of the monument. The sarsens were erected in two concentric arrangements – an inner horseshoe and an outer circle – and the bluestones were set up between them in a double arc.

About 200 and 300 years' later the central bluestones were rearranged to form a circle and inner oval, which again was altered to form a horseshoe. An avenue was also created at this time connecting Stonehenge with the river Avon.

As the land was virtually barren at this time, where did these megalithic stones, weighing several tons, come from? How could they have been transported with very primitive tools by man alone?

Four of the sarsens were adorned with hundreds of carvings depicting daggers and axe heads. Perhaps these axes were a symbol of power or status relating in some way to nearby burials. The whole monument, now in ruins, is aligned towards the sunrise on the Summer Solstice.

AVEBURY, WILTSHIRE, ENGLAND

Although Stonehenge is the most architecturally sophisticated prehistoric stone circle in the world, Avebury is the largest. Together with interrelated monuments they demonstrate Neolithic and Bronze Age ceremonial practices resulting from around 2000 years of continuous use and monument building between circa 3700 and 1600.

Avebury henge and stone circles are one of the greatest marvels of prehistoric Britain. The henge survives as a huge bank and ditch, and within it is the largest stone circle in Britain, originally of about 100 stones, which in turn enclose two smaller stone circles. These circles actually encompass the village of Avebury.

The massive henge is the largest prehistoric mound in Europe and demonstrates the outstanding engineering skills which we are used to created masterpieces of megalithic and earthen architecture. These sites would have been of major significance to those who created them by the huge amount of time and effort they represent. They provide in insight into the ceremonial and mortuary practices of the period.

THE MOAI OF EASTER ISLAND POLYNESIA

The average size of a Moai statue is 13 feet and weighs 14 tons. The Rapa Nui natives believed the spirit of the chieftain or important person would forever watch over the tribe and bring good fortune. Although these statues are commonly known as the 'Easter Island Heads', this is a misconception, as more recent excavation has revealed full bodies below the level of the surrounding earth, also when first discovered the statues were all lying down, having fallen over time.

Located on Easter Island, called Rapa Nui, these figures were said to have been carved between 1,250 and 1,500 CE by the Rapa Nui people, representing the deified ancestors of the population.

There have been 887 Moai statues discovered on the island, the largest being 33 feet tall! Again, how can these primitive people have moved them and where did the stone come from? They were carved from volcanic ash, red scoria, trachyte and basalt.

The name 'Easter Island' originated with the European explorer Jacob Roggeveen, who first discovered the island on Easter Sunday 1722.

EGYPTIAN PYRAMIDS

In Giza, just outside Cairo, the most famous of all pyramids rises from the floor of the desert. Built more than 4,500 years' ago, the pyramids at Giza are said to be monumental tombs where ancient queens and pharaohs were buried. But how did the Egyptians build them? The Great Pyramid consists of millions of precisely hewn stones weighing approximately two tons each. Even with the cranes and other heavy equipment we have today, building a pyramid as big as Pharoah Khufu's would be impossible; not only that but the astronomical configuration of the pyramids is said to align with the stars in Orion's belt. The Pyramid of Giza is aligned in the very centre of North, South, East and West. In the centre of the pyramid is a hidden chamber made of red granite, which can only be found 600 miles away. It is thought to have been built as a possible power plant, converting the energies of the Earth. Inside the pyramid is a channel where water is directed downwards, making the pyramid vibrate.

Many archaeologists think that it was not actually built for tombs, as none have been found. Egypt is not the only area where pyramids can be seen; pyramids appear in many other countries with equally fascinating and mystical stories attached to them.

THE SPHINX

The Sphinx is claimed to have been built between 2558 and 2532 BC. It is the oldest monumental structure in Egypt and one of the oldest in the world. The giant sphinx of Gaza is a statue of a mythical creature with a human head and the body of a lion. There are many found all over the world, though the Great Sphinx of Egypt is unmatched by the skill of its structure.

As it was built over 4,500 years' ago, no-one really knows why. It was built under the instruction of Pharaoh Khafre. There are secret tunnels and chambers still to be discovered beneath the sphinx, holding many further fascinating secrets. As yet only a few have been discovered.

TEOTIHUACAN MEXICO

Built more than 2,000 years' ago, Teotihuacan, meaning 'City of the Gods', is a sprawling, ancient city in Mexico. The Pyramid of the Sun rises up against an azure sky in Mexico City. Scientists suspect that over the centuries, a mix of cultures including Maya, Zapotec and Mixtee built this city, which could accommodate more than 100,000 people.

With its murals, tools, transportation system and evidence of advanced agricultural knowledge, Teotihuacan is considered more technically developed than should have been possible in pre-Aztec Mexico.

CHAPTER 5

Alien Abductions

Many people are convinced that not only an Alien race exists, but also that they visit our planet frequently. In fact, many claim to have had personal experiences that undoubtedly prove this to be true.

Steven Spielberg's influential film 'War of the Worlds' refers to direct contact between aliens and humans. In 1952 George Adamski claimed to have met a rather attractive Venusian in the Californian desert (Bartholomew & Howard 1998). He even claimed that he had been taken for a ride in her spaceship and wrote several best-selling books recounting his adventures.

The first alien abduction to receive worldwide attention is that of Barney and Betty Hills:

The thought that something was chasing them went through the minds of Betty and Barney Hills as they drove down the empty winding road in New Hampshire's

White Mountains. It was a night in September 1961 and they had not seen another car for several miles, though something, a strange light, followed them.

When they reached home in Portsmouth at dawn, they were both mystified and scared, and far from feeling relieved at arriving at, what should have been a place of safety, they felt dirty, their watches had stopped working, Barney's shoes were strangely scuffed and Betty's dress was ripped. There were two whole hours that they could not account for and had no knowledge of.

With the help of a psychiatrist, the couple eventually revealed, under hypnosis, a terrifying story. Grey beings with large eyes had walked them into a very large metal disc. Once inside the beings had examined the couple and erased their memories.

Sightings of strange lights and objects in the sky became the raw material for Hollywood movies, with plots of potential threats from extra-terrestrial beings. Since the 1940's and 50's, and perhaps even earlier, there have been UFO sightings all over our world; Africa, Asia, Australia, France, Canada, Portugal, Brazil, Spain, United Kingdom and the USA.

Pyramids

These are the known pyramids that have been discovered around the world:

- Saqqara, Egypt: Pyramid of Djoser
- Giza, Egypt: Great Pyramid of Khufu
- Giza, Egypt: Pyramid of Khafre
- Chavin de Huantar, Peru: Chavin Temple Complex
- Teotihuacan, Mexico : The Pyramid of the Sun
- Mereo, Sudan: The Nubian Pyramids
- Puebla, Mexico: Great Pyramid of Cholula
- Ur, Iraq: Ziggurat
- Peten, Guatemala: Mayan Pyramids of Tikal
- Rome, Italy: Pyramid of Cestius

We are so familiar with the pyramids of Egypt that we tend not to consciously acknowledge that around the world there are many more astounding and awesome structures. To try to fathom the means of construction completely dumbfounds us, the sheer size of the blocks customized to form these structures vastly outweighing the possibility of man to harness and lift them. The puzzle remains to this day as to how they managed it; alien intervention?!

Cloning

The Greys have been accused of abducting humans and of mutilating animals for the harnessing of organs etc. supposedly for the purpose of either cloning or producing a 'hybrid' entity. This obviously creates a degree of fear, not only of the abductions but also for the possible creation of some sort of grotesque being; beings that perhaps we have observed carved into the many megalithic structures and rock carvings around the world.

Imagine for example, an incredibly fit and battle hungry soldier/dictator with a view to annihilating a certain country and its people. An army of super-human specimens could be created who would be entirely dispensable, with no family ties, no homes and no ethnicity.

People could possibly clone themselves to produce body parts that have defects or are worn out. Tissue can even be taken from a dead person. Animals have been, and are, cloned to re-invent a loved animal. The first official cloning that we know of was of course 'Dolly the sheep'!

Dolly was important as she was the first mammal to be cloned from an adult cell. Her birth proved that specialized cells could be used to create an exact copy of the animal they came from. Dolly was a female Dorset sheep who lived from 1996 to 2003. She was cloned by British biologist Ian Wilmut of the Roslin Institute in Scotland. Her birth marked a milestone in science, dispelling protestations that adult mammals could not be cloned, and igniting furious debate concerning the many uses, and misuses of mammal cloning technology.

China's Pig/Monkey

Scientists in China are working to create human organs within pigs. The idea is that while waiting lists for human organ transplants grows, this method of growing human organs within pigs could offer a solution. Although the 'pig/monkey' hybrid proved unsuccessful, the pigs died within weeks of being born, it isn't likely to be the last we hear of it. However, raising pigs only to kill them for the use of implanted organs raises some rather serious ethical concerns.

CHAPTER 6

Crystal Skulls

In the late 19th century around a dozen carved skulls made of rock crystal appeared in both public and private collections around the world. Since then, the origin of the skulls has been subject of ongoing mystery and controversy. According to the people who claimed to have discovered the skulls, they date back thousands, or even tens of thousands of years, to ancient civilizations such as the Aztec, Toltec, Mixtec or Maya. Many of those who believe in the crystal skulls attribute them with natural powers, including healing properties and the power to expand a person's psychic abilities when holding or touching the skull.

Some are crystal clear, others of smoky or coloured quartz. Some are life size and beautifully carved, while others are smaller and less refined. All are believed to originate from Mexico and Central America. There are those who believe the skulls are a form of computer able to record energy and vibrations that occur around them. It is said that they contain the history of the world.

However, it cannot be proved one way or the other that these skulls are genuinely ancient, or perhaps carved by modern methods.

One of the crystal skulls is in the archives of the British Museum and was once owned by Tiffany & Co. of New York. Researchers believe a company partner bought it at an auction through a man named Eugene Boban who plays a central role in the skull's mystery. In major museum collections around the world you can find beautifully carved and haunting crystal skulls in all shapes and sizes. The smallest is just a simple amulet, while the largest is larger than a bowling ball.

For generations visitors to the museums have been captivated by their allure.

UFO Subterranean Bases

UFOs have been sighted hovering over the ocean and disappearing into the water. In a leaked US Navy recording of this incident, it was confirmed that the video was recorded by military personnel. Numerous sightings of UFOs have been reported by dozens of pilots flying across the Pacific Ocean.

Newly leaked videos show a UFO disappearing into the water. In another leaked video what appears to be a UFO flies around a Navy ship off the coast of San Diego before suddenly disappearing after flying into the water.

Roswell

The most universally known UFO incident in history is of course ROSWELL. Roswell was an unparalleled turning point for all mankind, because for the first time almost every man, woman and child on earth was faced with the possibility that we are not alone in the universe. In June 1947 Major Jesse Marcel, commander of the most technologically advanced bomb group in the world, discovered the crash site of a UFO in the New Mexico desert, following a record- breaking storm. From duty to his country, Major Marcel was to become the scapegoat for the largest cover-up in world history. What he saw would be a secret he would be instructed to keep for many years – knowledge about the crash itself, the body found, and the ensuing battle to keep the incident covered up by government and military factions. Roswell would be forever entwined, in not just Major Marcel's life, but that of his children and grandchildren for generations to come.

Today, Jesse Marcel III the grandson of Major Jesse Marcel, tells his grandfather's story and reveals what has continued to haunt his family for over sixty years – the legacy of Roswell.

Ley Lines: Earth's Energy Grid

A grid of earth's energies circles the globe, connecting sacred sites such as Stonehenge, the Egyptian Pyramids, and the Great Wall of China. If you plot these lines on a map a curious thing becomes apparent; many can be connected by straight lines. Were these monuments and sacred sites specifically formed at these locations to connect earth's energies along these 'ley lines'?

There has often been found special significance in the unusual landmarks and geological features surrounding them. High mountain peaks and majestic valleys might be viewed as sacred, while deep dark caverns have often been considered the domain of the underworld.

Our ancestors built and used prominent features in the landscapes as navigational points, including prehistoric standing stones, stone circles, barrows, mounds, hill forts and earthworks, ancient moats, old preformation churches, old cross-roads, prominent hilltops and fragments of old, straight tracks. Perhaps these 'walkways' were used for trade and to delineate direction in prehistoric times.

Rock and Cave Carvings

What is quite extraordinary is the fact that the symbols and sometimes grotesque figures depicted on rocks and in caves around our planet, appear to be identical though they have been constructed many thousands of miles apart. These carvings and also writings would seem to be of beings that might possibly have been visiting our planet millions of years' ago.

The Octopus

Something most bizarre is the octopus! This creature has three hearts and nine brains! Is it possible that it possesses extra-terrestrial DNA? It has something like 50,000 genes compared to a human who possesses approximately 25,000 genes. There is ample evidence therefore, that it evolved somewhere else! It seems that these creatures were brought here in their entirety and put into our oceans by other entities.

The brains of the octopus, instead of being in its head, are distributed around its body and also its arms. It can manipulate its body into any number of different shapes, therefore being able to imitate its prey or hide undetected. It is also highly intelligent. If any species were to survive to rule the world, it would be the octopus!

CHAPTER 7

OUR CONNECTION TO THE UNIVERSE

H ow are we connected to the Universe and the Stars? Most of the elements of our bodies were formed in stars over the course of billions of years and multiple star lifetimes. However, it is also possible that some of our hydrogen and lithium, which our bodies contain in very tiny trace elements, originated from the Big Bang.

For decades scientists have said humans are made of stardust, and now a new survey of the stars has proved just how true this is. Humans and the galaxy have approximately 97% of the same kind of atoms.

The Universe is endless in its beauty and wonder. When we look up at the stars or the moon, we feel a calming connection. In other words, through the connection with the Universe, we are able to obtain knowledge and feel that we belong. By gazing upwards towards the stars we realize that not only do we exist, but other things in the Universe also exist. While looking up, although we appear incredibly small, we rarely feel worthless, we become one with the beauty of it.

The Moon

Since the beginning of time humans have been observing the Moon and its changes and acknowledging our undeniable connection with its ebbs and flows. Our emotions, sleep, menstruation, and our love life have all been linked to the Moon.

The Moon exerts a strong gravitational pull which causes the changing of our tides in our oceans. This pull is at its strongest during the New Moon and Full Moon, subsequently we experience the highest and the lowest tides. Considering, as humans, we are made up of 70% water, it would make sense that as water beings, the Moon would have a similar impact on us. At the New Moon and the Full Moon, like the tides, our emotions and feelings are heightened. Our sleep can also be affected in that less sleep is experienced when the Moon is full compared to the rest of the month. It is believed that our internal biological rhythms may be linked to the phases of the Moon. This would obviously make us more irritable, impatient and stressed!

The Planets

All of us have a unique birth chart depicting exactly where each planet and constellation was in the sky at the moment of our birth. Every planet is associated with specific traits that impact on our individual character, moods, strengths and weaknesses. Each planet in our chart represents a facet of our personality. Each planet is linked to a specific sign of the zodiac.

To understand how the planets are affecting us we have to know where they are located at any given time. The planets that move relatively fast are – Mercury, Venus and Mars, as they are closer to the Earth, influencing short term issues in our everyday lives. The outer planets – Jupiter, Saturn, Neptune, Uranus and Pluto, take 7 years to move through the zodiac, so they are connected to large scale or generational events. Jupiter and Saturn govern interpersonal issues, while Uranus, Neptune and Pluto influence larger issues and those pertaining to society.

The Sun

The Sun represents our identity, ego and sense of self. The Sun is the brightest star in our solar system and symbolizes our core being, our will to live, and our creative force. Its movements govern important aspects of our personal lives, like our health, well-being and strength.

MERCURY

Mercury governs communication, intellect and awareness. This planet influences our ability to explain, to understand the world around us. Logic, teaching, reasoning and learning are within Mercury's capabilities. Mercury is quick moving and can make us feel restless.

VENUS

Venus is all about beauty, harmony and pleasure. Our emotional attachments, marriages, friendships and other relationships, are governed by Venus. The energy of Venus allows us to look attractive and to attract others. Socializing, empathy, the arts and luxury are all part of this planet's pleasurable domain.

JUPITER

Jupiter governs the realms of religion and philosophy, and to explore ideas. It can affect our sense of optimism and bring good luck into our lives.

SATURN

Saturn is the 'task master' of the heavens – demanding that we get to work, be disciplined and responsible. Saturn also governs old age, and the invaluable wisdom that comes with it.

URANUS

Uranus governs social change and technological advancement. Progressive ideas, new inventions, unconventional art, and large-scale intellectual ideas are all ruled by Uranus.

NEPTUNE

Dreams, mystery, illusion are governed by Neptune. It is tied very closely to our heightened awareness and our spirituality. Neptune strongly influences music and dance, poetry, theatre and film.

PLUTO

Pluto's energy influences hidden aspects of ourselves. Its connection to creation means it governs the reproductive system, but it has a sinister side representing obsession and crime.

CHAPTER 8

WHAT LIES BENEATH?

The Beings of Inner Earth, and the Crystal City

During an Arctic expedition in 1946 Admiral Richard Byrd makes a very extraordinary and dramatic discovery. He was the recipient of the Medal of Honour, the highest honour for Valour given by the United States, and was a pioneering American Aviator, polar explorer and organizer of polar logistics. Aircraft flights in which he served as a navigator lead across the Atlantic Ocean. Byrd was the first man to reach both the North Pole and the South Pole by air. He has been recognized for all his discoveries except for one; an ancient city *under* Antarctica.

It is during this time that a number of mysterious unidentified flying objects were said to have been seen. Modern UFO sightings became very frequent after the detonation of nuclear bombs on the Japanese cities of

Hiroshima and Nagasaki. It was as if some ancient beings had been disturbed by this, and they began to monitor us constantly. Do they share this planet and have been living here long before humanity emerged?

Admiral Byrd's story continues. He had been on several explorations before, but after the world war he was asked by the government to go on the largest exploration to Antarctica ever undertaken. Following this Admiral Byrd commanded more than 4,000 troops, warships and 'planes on this top secret expedition to the South Pole. The mission was named 'Operation High Jump' and was to last four months.

The mission was a huge success. It opened up the continent's interior for further scientific exploration. However, in the third month something extraordinary and unexpected happened that the government has kept from the public to this day.

Admiral Byrd discovered a crystal city under the earth, but the government suppressed the information, and only after his death did his son discover his diary in which Byrd narrated the incident.

While flying he discovered an underworld earth through the South Pole. As he flew over the Pole, suddenly he was looking at things that should not be there. The temperature was temperate. His squadron literally flew into the earth, where it turned into a lush green area, and he tells of how suddenly he started to see a shimmering rainbow city made of crystal. Suddenly his 'plane is taken control of and he sees flying disk-shaped objects around them that lead him to the ground, whereupon he is escorted into a cavernous type of area where he meets a being he refers to as 'the master' in his diary. The master tells him that they are highly disappointed in what humans are doing with nuclear weapons, and how they have recently destroyed Hiroshima and Nagasaki. They really are concerned about what is happening on the surface of the planet. They tell Admiral Byrd that they hope that humanity will ultimately stop this.

This account is particularly significant due to the fact that the modern UFO era began right after WWII and the detonation of the first atomic bomb. It has also been noted that a high number of UFO sightings have been reported within the vicinity of nuclear missile silos.

Admiral Byrd's story is in accordance with the stories that we hear from numerous accounts of extra-terrestrial beings that are very concerned about what humanity is doing with nuclear weapons. They are very concerned that not only are we going to destroy ourselves but could irreparably harm our planet, which is their world as well.

If Admiral Byrd's diary is authentic, does it reveal not only that there are highly advanced beings living inside the earth, but also that they are monitoring what happens on the surface? According to the diary, this incredible encounter Admiral Byrd was eager to share was, by order of the government, to remain *secret*, therefore he was unable to disclose his astounding discovery. On his return after this experience he was taken to a government compound, where he was told that he was *never* to speak of this publicly, and that everything he said was to remain classified.

China's Subterranean City

Archeologists have long been stunned by the underwater 'Lion City', a once thriving Chinese civilisation. Hidden in the depths of Qiandao Lake, China, lies a mysterious sunken city. A myriad of ornate temples, each intricately carved with script and perfectly preserved offers a tantalizing glimpse into China's Imperial past. The city, known as Shi Cheng, is 140 feet underwater and was built during the Eastern Han Dynasty, dating back to the 2nd century. Its name loosely translates to 'Lion City' and was once a thriving hub of commerce.

Only in recent years have its ancient splendours been discovered by researchers and explorers, who describe the space beneath them as a "unique underwater world". The ancient city was flooded as part of the Chinese government's 'Great Leap Forward' plan to make way for the country's first hydropower plant.

Are We Really Made of Stardust?

As a star burns through its fuel and begins to cool, the outward forces of pressure drop. When the pressure drops low enough in a massive star, gravity suddenly takes over and the star collapses in just seconds. This collapse produces the explosion called a supernova.

The periodic table of chemical elements organizes all discovered chemical elements in rows called periods, and columns called groups. Scientists use the periodic table to quickly refer to information pertaining to an element. The periodic table's arrangement also allows scientists to discern trends in element properties, including electro-negativity, ionization energy and atomic radius.

Stars that go supernova are responsible for creating many of the elements of the periodic table, including those that make up the human body.

It is 100% true that nearly all the elements in the human body were made in a star, and many have come through several supernovas. It is thought that the universe began 12 or 13 billion years' ago with the Big Bang. At that point only the lightest elements such as hydrogen, helium and miniscule amounts of lithium were incorporated.

Stars are immense objects. Over 99% of the mass in our solar system is in our Sun, and gravity squeezes them. Meanwhile, the burning inside a star creates energy which counteracts the squeeze of gravity, which is why our Sun is stable.

When stars die and lose their mass, all the elements that had been generated inside are swept into space. The next generation of stars form from those elements, burn, and are again swept out. This constant reprocessing of everything is called galactic chemical evolution.

If you combine every element made in a star in different ways, you can make species of gas, minerals and bigger things, such as asteroids, and from asteroids you can start making planets, and then start to make *water and other ingredients required for life* and then eventually – **us**!

Nazi Alien Technology

The Nazis possessed technology that was 100 years ahead of the allies. After being captured, many top scientists and psychiatrists of the elite Nazi regime admitted that an outside force assisted them, and that the 3rd Reich's ultimate mandate was to create 'the most powerful weapon' the world had ever seen. Hitler's UFOs is the story of the Nazis and the Aliens from outer space.

Nazi Germany was among the first countries in the world to develop an interest in flying saucers for their strategic significance. An airport hangar in Prague was turned into a research facility where engineers struggled to get their creations off the ground. Though they probably did not succeed, their interest in the subject has given UFOs a sense of mystique they have kept to this day.

The Lost Kingdom of Atlantis

Santorini has often been connected with Atlantis, the legendary kingdom that sank to the bottom of the sea, while it was at its zenith. It was said that the story of Atlantis revealed that it was a great and wonderful state which ruled over the islands and which owed its power to the civilization that had evolved there.

This story was told to an Athenian lawyer called Solon in 590 BC, while visiting Egypt, by a priest by the name of Sais.

The kingdom consisted of two islands, the 'larger' and the 'smaller', and there were ten cities. Of these only two were mentioned specifically, the 'Metropolis' and the 'Royal City'. The people of Atlantis launched an attack on Athens 900 years before Solon had spoken to the priest. The Athenians defeated them and liberated all the lands that Atlantis had conquered.

Later, Atlantis suffered a terrible earthquake and flood, causing it to sink in its entirety beneath the waves. Finds from the excavations at Akrotiri have led archaeologists to conclude that the lost kingdom of Atlantis was none other than Santorini. However, over time, as the myth was retold, experts have been inclined to believe that this might not be true, and Prof. Marinatos identified Atlantis with Minoan Crete. Perhaps Crete was the 'larger' island, the 'Royal City', while Santorini, with which Crete had ties, would have been the 'Metropolis' or 'smaller' island. However, we are still unsure. Was there such a place at all as Atlantis?

CHAPTER 9

Could We Live on Mars?

Caltech researchers used the Mars Reconnaissance Oribitor to determine that surface water left salt minerals behind as recently as 2 billion years' ago. Mars once rippled with rivers and ponds billions of years' ago, providing a potential habitat for microbial life.

As the planet's atmosphere thinned over time that water evaporated, leaving behind the frozen desert world that we observe today. Whilst exploring an ancient river delta in a crater on Mars, NASA's Perseverance Rover collected samples of two rocks that contained carbon-based molecules that could be remnants of past life. The rocks were formed several billions of years' ago when the crater was a lake, where life could definitely have existed.

DID LIFE ORIGINATE ON MARS?

Most scientists have assumed that life began here on our Earth. However, alternatively, the possibility that living cells arrived from space, strikes many people as absolutely impossible, and science fiction. Developments over the past decade have given new credibility to the idea that Earth's biosphere could have arisen from an extra-terrestrial seed!

Exploration Rovers corroborate previous beliefs that water has at least flowed on the Red Planet in the past. It is not unreasonable to assume that life existed on Mars and that people actually lived there, and perhaps still do!

Incidentally, did you know that humans grow two to three inches in height when living in space?

STRUCTURES ON MARS

With data and photography gathered from the afore-mentioned Rovers exploring the surface of Mars, various quite extraordinary structures have been seen, such as a human statue, a Buddha statue and even a cross and a sphynx. This may be a trick of the eye, though experts are not convinced. There are also structures resembling pyramids which seem to be aligned with stars in the galaxy.

Science fiction has become science fact. Is there a space programme on Mars? Is there a top-secret programme that the public does not know about? A base on Mars. Why would NASA try to hide this?

DR VON BRAUN'S PREDICTION

A book that was written 70 years' ago by Dr. von Braun, predicted that a man called Elon would attempt to colonize other planets, and specifically Mars. Dr. von Braun wrote the book in 1948 while at Ft. Bliss, Texas, called 'Marsprojekt'. The science fiction novel was published in German, after which it appeared later published in English.

Dr. von Braun was one of the most influential engineers of the 20th century and served as the first director of Marshall Space Flight Center in Huntsville. He was a key figure in the development of America's space programme, which led to the historic accomplishment of landing humans on the moon. He also envisaged a manned trip to Mars following the excursion to the Moon.

Seventy years later Elon Musk (whom we know from Social Media) is capturing much interest for space travel in saying he is open about his wish to explore the worlds, recently expressing that he wants to "make humanity a multi-planet species". Elon Musk is one of several billionaires with plans to colonize the Red Planet within the next few decades. His company SpaceX recently became the first private outfit to launch NASA astronauts into space. And while SpaceX's reusable rockets have only reached Earth's orbit so far, the Californian company predict that future craft will travel much further.

Trans Humans

THE CYBORG STORY

After a horrific accident left very little of his son Victor's body intact, Dr. Silas Stone used all his advanced scientific knowledge to save his only child's life, and to rebuild him into a superior being, one that was arguably more machine than man. Victor became part man and part machine – a Cyborg.

As a Cyborg, Victor was now far stronger than the average person, could interact with computers, and emit various types of energy that made him a formidable fighter. Although he ultimately chose the life of a super-hero, he never fully acclimatised to being only partially human, and was left with a melancholy within him, mourning for his past life.

We are already replacing organs and body parts with man-made prosthetics and alien donation organs; building a new generation of humans. Fertilized eggs can now be altered, if defective, to produce a healthy embryo. We are already on the road towards 'designer' babies.

Japanese scientists are working on producing the perfect child. They are experimenting with extracting DNA from as many as three different sources, therefore creating a perfect embryo. They are not the first to do this. We could eventually become a super-intelligent species.

The brain can even be altered to advance the human IQ. It is suggested that by 2045 we may well be able to live without limit. Is dying something we have to do? The quest for immortality has been going on for centuries, with potent 'elixirs' ingested to potentially prolong life. Perhaps in the future with the right pill we could achieve this!

Reverse ageing in mice has been done, so the next step is in humans. We are already implanting pacemakers, cochlea implants, organs and replacing bones etc. In the future the power of our thoughts may well control technology.

It will not be long before our intelligence has advanced to a point where we will no longer inhabit the Earth. Are we being guided into a new future, and is all this research, space flights and exploration merely preparing us for life elsewhere? There is no doubt about it, *we are going to have to change*.

The Bermuda Triangle

The Bermuda Triangle is a section of the North Atlantic Ocean off North America in which more than 50 ships and 20 aeroplanes are said to have mysteriously disappeared. The area has a vaguely triangular shape marked by the Atlantic coast of Florida in the United States, Bermuda and the Greater Antilles. Reports of unexplained occurrences in the region date back to the mid 19th century. Some ships have been found like 'ghost ships' completely abandoned for no apparent reason, others transmitted no distress signals and were never heard of again. Aircraft have vanished without trace, and rescue missions also have never been found, leaving no wreckage.

A popular theory, amongst many, is that the missing vessels were felled by huge 100 foot waves, which are known to abound in that area, destroying any visible evidence of a ship or 'plane.

When Christopher Columbus sailed through the area on his first voyage to the New World, he reported that a great flame of fire (probably a meteor) crashed into the sea one night and that a strange light appeared in the distance a few weeks later. He also wrote of erratic compass readings. A pattern allegedly began forming in which vessels traversing the Bermuda Triangle would either disappear or be found abandoned.

In 1945 an American Navy mission carrying 14 men, known as 'Flight 19', got incredibly lost while flying over the area. Their compasses mal-functioned, and after flying aimlessly until they ran out of fuel, were forced to ditch at sea. That same day a rescue 'plane with a 13-man crew also completely disappeared. After a massive weeks-long search failed to turn up any evidence, the official Navy report declared that it was "as if they had flown to Mars".

CHAPTER 10

Mysteries of Antarctica

The Great White Continent is the most baffling and unexplained corner of the Earth, and despite the dedicated efforts of scientists and explorers around the world Antarctica holds on to its secrets.

There are lakes and rivers teaming with life beneath the ice. In 2014 Lake Whillans, the third largest lake on the continent which lies 2,500 feet beneath the West Antarctic Ice Sheet, was shown to contain nearly 4,000 different microbial species.

Beneath its icy surface scientists are beginning to discover vast networks of complex life forms never seen anywhere on the planet before. Most people don't know much more about Antarctica's unique wildlife other than the seals and penguins that live on the surface, but over 90% of Antarctica's species are found on the sea floor and over half of those are found nowhere else on Earth. There could be thousands more species waiting to be discovered.

In the McMurdo Dry Valley, a bright crimson, five-storey, blood-coloured waterfall tumbles out of Taylor Glacier into Lake Bonney. It looks like a rush of blood from a dreadful wound in the ice, but scientists have discovered that the water that feeds Blood Falls was once a salty lake that is now cut off from the atmosphere due to the formation of glaciers on top of the lake. The water is extremely rich in iron and devoid of oxygen and sunlight. As the iron-rich water seeps through a fissure in the glacier and comes into contact with the air, the iron oxidises and rusts, staining the water blood red! A hole the size of Ireland opened up in Antarctica in 2017. Known as a polynya, the hole is nothing new except that with a span of 78,000 square kilometres it is the largest hole to be discovered since the 1970's, and the first one to open in 40 years.

Despite its freezing temperature Antarctica is home to a number of volcanoes. There are four volcanoes on Ross Island, although all our inactive except Mount Erebus, which actually increased in activity in the last 30 years.

Mount Erebus is an extreme natural wonder, with liquid magma and ancient lava lakes that have been boiling for around 1.3 million years. It is the world's southernmost active volcano and Antarctica's second highest volcano reaching a height of 3,800 metres.

Although meteorites can fall all over the earth, they are easier to find in Antarctica as the cold, dry conditions preserve the rocky fragments. They are almost always extra-terrestrial rocks, as few rocks actually form naturally on the ice sheets of Antarctica.

From elongated skulls and strange pyramids, to alien spaceships, bizarre structures and a giant staircase, many people believe that Antarctica was once inhabited by extra-terrestrial life (and perhaps still is!). The mystery of Antarctica continues deep below its surface where no-one has gone before. Yet another theory regarding the Lost City of Atlantis is that it is buried in the ice of Antarctica. It is quite possible that a civilisation existed in Antarctica when the climate was a warm, tropical region, but it is yet to be proven.

It is also theorised that the Nazis used underground Antarctica as a secret hideaway, and some people believe that Hitler fled there after the war. Hitler had a passion for the occult and was searching for something in Antarctica. The Nazis built a station there, though it was abandoned 70 years after the crew were poisoned by polar bear meat!

A massive slab of ice in Antarctica is singing! The Ross Ice Shelf is the largest ice shelf in Antarctica, being several hundred metres thick and covering an area over 500,000 square kilometres. Scientists have recently discovered that the Ross Ice Shelf sings an eerie melody, caused by the winds that blow across the snow dunes. The winds create surface vibrations and almost non-stop seismic tones. The song, although not audible to human ears, was discovered by accident after seismic sensors were installed on the ice shelf to observe other behaviours. Scientists have since discovered that the song changes in response to the environment, such as melting ice or storms shifting the snow.

Russian Cosmonaut
Sightings of Angels

In July 1984, Russian cosmonauts aboard the Soviet Space Station Soyuz 7 were on day 155 of their mission.

According to Commander Oleg Atkov and cosmonauts Vladimir Solovyov and Leonid Kizim, the space station was suddenly bathed in a mesmerizing orange light. It appeared to enter from outside the space station and seemed to bleed through an absolutely opaque wall.

For a short time, the light was so bright that it blinded the crew. When their vision returned, each one looked out of the portholes for the source of the light, looking for a possible explosion. They knew that the Soyuz 7 had suffered fires in the past, but what the crew saw was more incomprehensible than the orange light!

All of the cosmonauts reported seeing the faces of seven angels who were hovering just outside the space station. They told ground control they were humanoid in appearance, with faces and bodies resembling humans, but they had wings and halos. These beings kept pace with the space station for 10 minutes before vanishing.

On day 167, the crew were then joined by another team of three from the Soyuz T-12 space craft Svetlana Savitskaya, Igor Volk and Vladimir Dzhanibekov. Shortly after their arrival the Soyuz 7 was once again bathed in this warm orange light. Then, like clockwork, they immediately looked out of the portholes to find, once again, these angelic beings. They were reportedly the size of an airliner, according to the cosmonauts.

This incident was deemed 'top secret' by the old Soviet Union and the crew were cautioned not to speak of the event publicly. As the whole crew reported seeing a 'smiling angel' this encounter could not be put down to fatigue due to an extended stay in space. The crew went on to stay in the vessel for a record-breaking 237 days before abandoning it.

Rudloe Manor, Wiltshire – England's Area 51

In the Southwest of England in the county of Wiltshire is a former RAF base called Rudloe Manor. At first glance it would seem to be any other quaint English manor house, but deep beneath the structure lies a vast network of underground tunnels and chambers. Contained within their walls is a closely kept secret. For years the RAF's secret service worked at Rudloe Manor across espionage and counterintelligence operations, but also something else - UFO investigations. This was consistently denied by the MOD, but in 2007, during a release of classified files from the National Archives, it was confirmed that the site was, in fact, the centre for UFO investigations in the 1950's.

Shortly before the files were released the MOD announced that Rudloe was no longer in use, but today the location is still fenced off, monitored by cameras and guarded by dogs. *What are they doing?*

Pilots' UFO Encounters

Although RAF personnel had reported seeing lights following their aircraft from as early as March 1942, there were similar sightings involving RAF bomber crews over the Balkans during the first week of October 1944. At the time, these were wrongly believed to be Messerschmitt Me 163 rocket-powered interceptors which did not operate at night.

The bulk of the sightings started happening in the last week of November 1944 when pilots flying over Western Europe by night reported seeing fast-moving round glowing objects following their aircraft. These were described as varying in colour, fiery, glowing red, white and orange. Some pilots described them as resembling Christmas tree lights and reported that they seemed to be toying with them, making wild turns before simply vanishing. Pilots and aircrew reported that the objects flew together in formation with their aircraft and behaved as though they were under intelligent control, though never displayed any hostile behaviour. However, any attempt from the aircrew to attack with weapons proved useless, as they could not be out manoeuvred or shot down, there ammunition literally bouncing off the alien craft and having no effect at all.

The phenomenon was so widespread that the military took the sightings seriously suspecting that these mysterious sightings might be secret German weapons, but further investigation revealed that both German and Japanese pilots were all reporting similar sightings.

Similar sightings are being reported around the world. *What do they want?*

Uluru or Ayers Rock, Australia

Ayers Rock, or Uluru is a sacred site and is seen as a resting place for ancient spirits, giving it a religious status. There has been human activity at the site in Australia's Northern Territory for 10,000 years according to archaeologists, who believe the rock was formed more than 60,000 years' ago. It was discovered in 1873 by explorer William Gosse, who then named it after the Chief Secretary of Southern Australia Sir Henry Ayers.

The Uluru translates as 'Great Pebble'. The Anangu people believe in its spiritual significance, and one can observe the rock changing colour throughout the day, and glowing red at sunrise and sunset. The Anangu people tell of Dreamland Stories explaining how the Aboriginals created their existence at Uluru, believing that they came originally from stardust.

The Anangu people have been striving for years to put a stop to tourists climbing on the rock and have put up signs which read "This is our home. Please do not climb". The rock is home to a variety of wildlife, with 21 native mammals currently living on Uluru, while others have been recently introduced.

The Dreamtime refers both to an era before time during which the present was formed, and to a constant other reality where spirits of the living exist eternally. It is believed that several mythical beings created the world through a series of songs. The songs contain instructions for daily life and details of the journeys that the creators took in forming the Earth. These songs refer to real places in Australia and contribute to the sacredness of these places. They believe that these land forms are a direct result of creators' actions "they are visible to show that the ancestral beings still exist".

For white Australians Ayers Rock represents an earthly attachment to the bush, a reminder of their country origins and their place in it. Because Uluru is of immense importance to both Aboriginals and white Australians a compromise has now been reached regarding accessibility and tourists have now been given permission to climb the rock. For the Aborigines, compromise reached with the government now only allows them to hold ceremonies at certain times of the year.

The Anangu people refer to the rock as "the naval of the Earth".

The Blue Mountains of Australia

The Blue Mountains are a ridge of mountains in New South Wales. UFO sightings over the Blue Mountains have become prolific and people have been known to disappear completely, though those who have not have returned with bizarre stories relating to their experiences. There have, in fact, been several alien abductions in Australia and around the world; abductees telling stories of being placed on a table, and being subjected to internal and external examinations, tissue etc. being taken and implants inserted under the skin, later to be extracted, examined, and found to be roughly the size of a grain of rice. What these implants are actually for has not yet been determined, and the message that they carry remains a mystery.

For countless generations Aboriginal people have shared the Blue Mountains land as their seasonal home, hunting ground, and spiritual and ceremonial place. The spirit of the land speaks through their ancestors, the water, the trees, the birds and animals, with memories passed on from one generation to the next.

The Aboriginals passed through the Blue Mountains on ancient access routes used for trade, ceremony and travel. They collected food from plants, hunted animals using every part of the animal for food, clothing, weapons and tools. They understood how to preserve the natural environment by only taking what they needed and using everything they took.

With colonisation came disease, and the Aboriginal people were devastated by the impact of smallpox and whooping cough.

Wormholes and Black Holes in Space

A Wormhole is theoretically a tunnel between two distant points in our universe that cuts the travel time from one point to another. Instead of travelling from many millions of years from one galaxy to another, with the right conditions one could use a Wormhole to reduce travel time down to perhaps hours or minutes.

In the early days of research into Black Holes physicists did not know if these strange and bizarre objects existed in the real world. However, over the years, evidence has accumulated and attest to the fact that Black Holes are very real, and even exist in our galaxy.

Wormholes, those fantastical tunnels to the other side of the universe hang in the same sort of balance, and if they really are out there in our cosmos, could humans possibly use them for incredible journeys? The original idea of a Wormhole came from the physicist Albert Einstein and Nathan Rosen. Together they studied equations that led them to believe and describe the inescapable pocket of space we call a Black Hole. Einstein and Rosen discovered that, theoretically at least, a Black Hole's surface might work as a bridge connecting to a second patch of space.

Our Extended Brain

Telepathy is defined as "the communication of impressions of any kind from one mind to another, independently of the recognized channels of sense". Over the last 70 years research has supported the reality of telepathy. This phenomenon has had implications, not only in the cognitive sciences, but also in the field of biological and healing sciences.

It has long been assumed that conscious intention affects living systems across any distance. Prayers, healing energy, and similar methods have for a long time been a part of medicine. Will this be our language in the future?

Extrasensory perception (ESP) refers to the aforementioned or '6th sense', and one that we are actually quite familiar with in a small way, sensing something is wrong, sensing an atmosphere, sensing someone we cannot see looking at us etc. Many studies have demonstrated that we can 'read' other people's minds. In fact, we can analyse the intentions and emotions of others automatically.

Telepathy is not solely a human ability, animals also are predisposed to the transfer of thoughts. Flocks of birds will turn seemingly automatically or wheel together in the sky. This quick action from all birds at the same time is thought to be similar to telepathy.

Our brains are wired to pick up intentions and emotions in others, and we all have the capacity for telepathy, though some of us may be more susceptible to its subtle aspects than others.

CHAPTER 11

Chakras

Our body is more than just physical and mental, it is also a system of chakras. Chakra is a Sanskrit word that means wheel or cycle. There are seven main chakras situated along the spine, from the base of your spine to the crown of your head.

Chakras are thought to provide energy that facilitates your organs, mind and intellect to work at their best possible level to form balance and harmony.

THE SEVEN CHAKRAS

The Root Chakra – Muladhara
The Root chakra, or Muladhara in Sanskrit, is the first and primary chakra, located at the base of the spine. It is linked with the colour Red and the element Earth. This chakra affects how you connect to the world and controls feelings of survival, ambition, dependency, and stability. As the primary

source of energy, its imbalance can lead to feelings of deep fear and insecurity, and cause feelings of frustration and lack of purpose.

When the chakra is balanced, it creates feelings of security, positivity, energy, independence and strength.

The Sacral Chakra – Svadhishthana

Below the naval, the Sacral chakra radiates the colour Orange and represents the element of water. It is considered to be responsible for sexuality, creativity, intuitiveness, self-worth, compassion and adaptability. When this chakra is unstable, it causes lack of creativity.

The Solar Plexus Chakra -Manipura Chakra

The Solar Plexus Chakra, known as the Manipura Chakra is the third chakra in the 7 Chakra system. It is situated just below the ribcage and radiates the colour Yellow. 'Mani' means the shining gem and 'pura' means the place; it is the energy centre of fire. This energy centre governs our ability to be confident, assertive and to make decisions from a place of inner wisdom. It is also the key to unlocking our personal power and building a strong sense of self. However, when this centre is off balance, we may experience feelings of insecurity, self doubt and a lack of direction in life.

The Heart Chakra - Anahata

The Heart chakra is a link to compassion, trust, passion, and love for self and others, and the colour associated with it is a warm glowing Green. Across the world the colour green has multiple cultural, social and spiritual meanings. When the Anahata chakra is off balance, it causes anger, lack of trust, anxiety, jealousy, fear and moodiness. An over-active Heart chakra can lead to high blood pressure, heart palpitations and further heart problems.

The Throat Chakra - Vishuddha

Vishuddha controls the neck, mouth, tongue and other parts of the throat area. The Throat chakra's colour is Blue, and its element is ether. This chakra is connected with self-expression, communication and confidence. A balanced Throat chakra regulates the flow of hormones and helps inner thoughts to be spoken positively.

The Third Eye Chakra – Ajna

The Third Eye or Ajna chakra sits between the eyebrows. It has no elemental association but is represented by the colour Indigo. It controls our intellect, intuition, wisdom and spiritual power. An open and balanced Third Eye chakra allows us to connect with this world and beyond. An underactive Third Eye manifests in headaches, possible migraine, or blurry vision. The Third Eye is believed to free us from earthly attachments.

The Crown Chakra – Sahastrara

Sahastrara, the Crown chakra, is at the top of the head, the highest of the seven main chakras. Its colour is Violet or

White. Also known as "thousand petal lotus" chakra, it is considered the most spiritual of the central chakras.

Opening the Crown chakra connects a person to their higher self, being the place of spirituality and enlightenment. It is connected to inner wisdom and the cosmos. When unbalanced it is thought to manifest depression, disconnection from the outside world, frustration and destructive emotions.

The Giants of Sardinia

On the Italian island of Sardinia researchers and archaeologists have made a massive discovery! They have uncovered two huge torsos belonging to a group of millenia-old sculptures known as the 'giants of Mont'e Parma'.

In 1974 a group of farmers, whilst ploughing their fields, dug up the first of the stone figures. Most remarkable were their faces, with deep set eyes and angular features, but even more remarkable was their height, with the sculptures standing at more than seven feet tall.

Researchers believe they belong to the Nuragic people, who inhabited the island between the 11th and 8th centuries BC. These people built more than 7,000 distinctive beehive-shaped megalithic structures known as Nuraghi, which can be found dotting the island, and lived over 4,000 years' ago. Sixteen figures have been found to date, some being housed in the Civic Museum in Cabras.

Based on the shields carved around their bodies, the newest finds are thought to be boxers, and will have to be carefully removed before archaeologists can study them fully. They have found over 5,000 fragments and they seem to represent men of war such as archers, boxers etc. They approach over a ton in weight and are utterly unique.

The reason these statues were constructed at this enormous height seemed to be because they were carved in the image of the people of that race. It is strange that the statues have been purposely buried in graves, as though they were ancestors. There are stories of giants all over the island.

Could these extraordinary gigantic figures really represent a genuine civilization who inhabited the island thousands of years ago? According to recent estimates, fragments have been found totalling forty-four statues. Twenty-five have already been restored and assembled in addition to thirteen Nuraghi models.

Remote viewing

Remote viewing is built into every one of us, though we may not be aware of it. We may well be using it without realizing it is happening.

If the scales of perception fell from our eyes, we would see everything as it really is, 'infinite'. **William Blake**

Remote viewing is the ability to envisage a distant location, person or event using clairvoyance. It is also sometimes called 'anomalous cognition' or second sight (third eye/sixth sense). Many of us experience this as an intuitive flash of insight that turns out to be correct. This ability seems to be present in the human population in varying degrees, rather like the ability, or lack of it, to play an instrument well or carry a tune.

It is possible that in the future this ability will eventually be enhanced, and we will be conversant in using it with ease.

Men In Black

The Men in Black are purported to be men dressed in black suits who claim to be government agents, who interrogate, threaten and allegedly memory-wipe, and sometimes even assassinate witnesses of UFO sightings to silence them from making public what they have seen.

There have been several alleged encounters with the Men in Black, their presence having been reported by UFO researchers and witnesses to their existence.

****

ENDNOTE

---

*H*aving traversed the world in this book, we come back automatically to Leonardo da Vinci. Was he intended to pass a message to future generations?

Music Hidden in The Last Supper

We are led to believe that da Vinci hid messages within his paintings, and there may be one that definitely stands out as plausible. MUSIC! Hidden in da Vinci's painting of The Last Supper, musical notes have been detected.

In 2007, a computer technician and musician named Giovanni Maria Pala discovered a hidden melody within da Vinci's painting of The Last Supper. The melody is slow and dirge-like, and is performed on a pipe organ, that being the most popular instrument of religious music during Leonardo's lifetime.

As Leonardo was renowned for writing from right to left, the melody begins on the right and flows to the left. Through his research, Pala discovered that many aspects of the painting fell in line with a musical staff. Each hand in the painting appeared to fit a note. Below the hands Pala found that the loaves of bread were also part of the design. Pala suggested that the artist intentionally used hands and bread as Christian symbols. The bread representing the body of Christ and the hands representing the occurrence of transubstantiation. The fact that they are all placed in precise intonation supports the theory that they were intended as musical notes.

Pythagorus discovered that everything in the universe resonates to 'music' and that there is 'harmony' in all things.

Could it be that Leonardo believed our connection to another world might be through music?

Inevitably therefore, and all things considered, we have to come to the conclusion that

WE ARE NOT ALONE! WE HAVE NEVER BEEN ALONE!

BV - #0154 - 041223 - C0 - 203/133/6 - PB - 9781916572386 - Gloss Lamination